How to be a Repo Man

A Complete
Recovery Agency
Operation Guide

James O'Reilly

© 2013 JAMES O'REILLY
& HIRED GUN PUBLICATIONS

HIREDGUNPUB.COM

The Pretext Play Book
By James O'Reilly

Find my pretext collection on Amazon at

http://bit.ly/pretextplay

The Most Useful Websites
Valerie McGilvrey

A collection of the most useful websites for small business & entrepreneurs giving ease to the operation of ownership.

http://bit.ly/mostuseful

For Cynthia

100% of the profit of this book is going to my daughter's law degree. If you enjoy it and find it an asset to your investigation tool box please let other investigators know about it so that they can have it in their tool box and my daughter can be a great lawyer.

Copyright & Disclaimer

This publication is not intended to replace nor be a substitute for any official procedural material issued by your agency of employment nor other official government source. Hired Gun Publications, the author and any associated advisors have made all possible efforts to ensure the accuracy and thoroughness of the information provided herein, but accept no liability whatsoever for injury, legal action or other adverse results following the application or adoption of the information contained. This is not legal advice and you should consult with an attorney regarding legal matters.

The opinions expressed in this book are solely the opinions of the author and do not represent the opinions or thoughts of the publisher. The author has represented and warranted full ownership and legal right to publish all materials in this book.

No part of this book may be reproduced or transmitted in any form or by any means electronically or mechanically including photocopying, recording or by any information storage and retrieval system, without permission in writing from the publisher. permissions@hiredgunpub.com

This publication is designed to provide general information in regard to the subject matter covered. It is sold with the understanding that the publisher is not engaged in rendering legal services. Although prepared by professionals, this publication should not be utilized as a substitute for professional service in specific situations. If legal advice or other expert assistance is required, the service of a professional should be sought.

Copyright © 2013, 2014 Hired Gun Publications & James O'Reilly
ISBN: 9781301656806
ISBN-13: 978-1490384900
ISBN-10: 1490384901

Dear Repo Man,

September 16, 2014

Because of the incredible response from people getting ready to organize their own repossession agency I decided to make some changes to this book updating it with some new ideas, information and happenings in the recovery industry.

I will maintain that this is solely my opinion in this book and I have not been paid to promote or suppress any service or company that relates to the repossession and recovery industry.

First of all, I'm selling the print copy at cost. I've reduced the type and page count which of course makes the paperback look tiny but since I had so many folks tell me the book is on the wish list I was compelled to do so. I want to make sure you have good info when you want it.

Second, the e-book version available everywhere you can buy e-books will either be one dollar or free. You won't need an e-reader to download the book from my site, HiredGunPub.com in PDF format.

To replace the lack of financial support I'll receive from royalties I have a few links that give me perks when you get an account. Since they are all industry related I'll explain those at the end of the book. These are things you need anyway such as trap lines.

And of course, the very best thing you can do for me is let people know you have received some good knowledge because of this book. Since I've opted to give it free to all who wish I have also opened the idea of a forum on my blog site.
If you have tips or ideas you would like to share with others please send me an email and I'll expeditiously post it on the site and will also put it in this book giving you credit with your email.

A major part of my success after retiring from law enforcement was to connect and network with other people that are in the same business.

It's not what you know but who you know. And it pays to know lots of people. In the forum I hope to create a directory where you can list your company information so people can find you.

Please hop over to HiredGunPub.com and enter your email address so that you can get updates as to when these things get implemented and when this book gets updated so you can download the newest copy.

Table of Contents

18...**Introduction**

21...**Business Structure**

26...**Repo TV Shows**

29...**Field Checks**

33...**Equipment**

38...**Insurance**

49...**Paper Work**

58...**Associations**

61...**Laws**

68...**DTPA and Pretexting**

71...**Personal Property**

74...**Releasing Collateral**

78...**Why Operation Repo is Bad**

81...**Stages of a Repo**

84...**Getting the Repo vs. Getting the Key**

88...**Dashboard Cams**

91...**GPS**

97...**Skip Trace**

103...**Impersonating a Police Officer**

107...**Trap-lines**

111...**Bail Outs**

113...**Repo Tools**

117...**Forms**

123...**Repo Laws by State**

134...**Recommended Reading**

137...**Helpful Websites**

140...**Glossary**

Introduction

So, you want to be a repo man. The best way to learn the business and be the best repo man in your area is to work for another repo company, if only for a short while. The immediate lessons learned are how to use the software programs and all of the very important front office matters.

I refer to the term "front office" meaning the behind the scenes work that takes place. Like getting updates from repo drivers that are working on an account and giving that update to the client that has the lien on the vehicle you're looking for. Also dealing with vendors and learning boundaries as pertaining to what to expect from them and terms of doing businesses you should agree to.

Just because you read it in this book doesn't mean it's so in your state. You must verify what your state and county repossession laws and requirements are. Repossessions are enforcing a financial interest on a loan by recovering what is called collateral. FDCPA subsection 1692 (a) (6) states that any agency that is enforcing a security interest is governed by this law. This does include repossession agency.

Regardless of the agreement to collect money for the lien holder, recovery of secured collateral is enforcing a security interest. Collateral is the property that is secured in the loan and would be a car, truck, boat, four-wheeler, 18-wheeler, plane or train. Mobile homes and small buildings can also be repossessed.

Anything that you can put your hands on that has a contract; verbal or written is secured collateral. That collateral securing the loan means that having possession of that item requires timely payments. Hence the saying, "If they don't pay, we take it away."

Many states in the U.S. are "self-help" states, which means that the lien holder has the right to repo secured property without judicial process, and in many states, no notification to the debtor is required (considering any notification could cause a debtor to hide a car).

A lien holder can go seek out and take back financed property without hiring an attorney and suing the debtor for the property. In some cases the property can be sold on auction and applied to the final balance of a contract.

Recovery is the only remedy that a credit grantor has to prevent a total loss. After the property is repossessed, if the debtor is working a job in a state that allows wage garnishment for judgments, the lien holder can garnish the debtor's wages until the loan is completely paid off.

Business Structure

How much will you make as a repo man? That answer solely lies in your figures at the end of the month. Experience will teach that you have to take the good with the bad. Investigation efforts can sometimes take many months to yield positive results and since most recovery companies offer their services on a contingent basis, your bottom line will vary month to month.

All of the leg work that goes into one account may not give you a pay day right away either. The stress of barely making as a repo man and great success are weighed by the volume of assignments. In a larger mix you will get various ways to bill your clients.

You could consider giving a discount for an assignment called a voluntary surrender. All you would have to do is drive out and pick up the vehicle and continue to process it as you would every other unit you repo. The discount comes as an incentive for that lien holder to call you, and not another repo man, when a debtor is turning over their vehicle to the lender.

Recovery fees vary from one region to another. What could be a $250.00 repo fee in one city would easily be a $650.00 in another. Prices are based on competition and experience. If you carry a one million dollar insurance policy, there is no way you would make a huge profit (or any profit at all) on a $250.00 repo fee. In the same turn, a client would stay with a company that has excellent insurance coverage.

The bigger the collateral, the bigger the repo fee. RV's pay an average of $800.00 to $2000.00. If you are uncertain of what fee to charge just pick up the phone and start calling other repo companies pretending to be a potential client with that type of collateral to be repossessed. You'll get quotes that give you fuel surcharges and mileage costs but you'll insight on the way it should be done.

These extras could come in the form of finder's fees paid to associates or expensive locates done by outside skip trace services or investigators in another state where the debtor is suspected to travel to.

Close fees would be paid in the event the collateral is recovered by another means or the lender accepts payment from the debtor. These fees can range from a full repo fee to a lesser fee that covers your in-house expenses for hunting the repo. When you first start out in business and are reaching out to potential clients a common mistake is to undercut the competition by coming in with a lower price.

Some of the different ways you can bill a client is a skip trace fee, involuntary repossession fee, mileage (usually a specific dollar amount per mile), close fees, transportation fee and additional storage fees (billed at a daily rate with the first ten days free). Another contract that is a gamble on hard to find skips is called a 50/50.

This contract gives your company 50% of the sale of the vehicle on auction. Dealing with high value collateral makes this contract worth all the extra work. Basically a lender will go for this contract if a vehicle has been out for repo from six months to a year and thought to be in good condition.

The bigger paycheck will help you justify spending additional funds spent in the location and recovery. The client knows you're going to go all out to get the unit picked up because you'll have a bigger paycheck at the end of the deal.

My personal advice to you is not to do this: Don't agree to take a volume of repo work that no one else has been able to find at a lower price. If a repo has been out for more than six months you can pretty well assume that the account has been beat to death by a long line of other repo companies.

You'll be just another knock on the door that gets ignored.

You also have no guarantee that the deal is not double assigned either. This means that you could make one positive move that convinces a debtor to surrender a car and then the other repo company be there at the right place at the right time and take your payday from you. I've also seen lien holders lie about how the collateral was recovered to get out of paying a close fee.

For instance, if you make a deal for no close fees if the unit is located in a mechanic's garage, or an impound lot. Be wary and require proof such as a paid invoice, name of the shop and impound notice. You can call the shop to verify the details that you are given. Make is a company policy to verify so that the proof is given without grievance on every occurrence.

Another twist to doing business with no close fee's is that you bust your chops to make contact regularly and get the unit out of the garage and then those folks get a income tax return check and run in and pay up to date.

This is getting the same result from your effort for the client. If that client accepts payment then they should pay your full repo fee and additional expenses. You shouldn't get punished for the company's decision to take money and not hold out for recovery. The finance company was apparently satisfied so the reward would be exactly the same.

Repo TV Shows

You'll read my attitude about repossession shows in this book and in other places. You have to know these shows are so corny and outright ridiculous. I could be repetitive here but if you're reading this book because you think being a repo man is cool like on TV. It's not.

Its hard work and it's dangerous. Any job is tricky when you're dealing with people that fight hard to keep a vehicle in tough times knowing they can't run out and get another one tomorrow.

The recovery shows are for entertainment only and they don't create show scripts that include law abiding actions. Such has a repossessor putting his hands on a person and throwing them off of an ATV. That's jail time in real life. It's looks good on television but that's what it's for on TV. Entertainment only.

A very good example is that the Lizard Lick cast was paid to appear at a repossession convention by a huge nationwide lien holder and the repo company owners who attended the convention banded together as a group and demanded that they be removed from the building. They were forced to leave the convention.

I wasn't there and I don't know exactly how it happened but it was a huge scene. The reason why is that Lizard Lick does not show good ethical business operations and does not represent the true integrity of law abiding repossession agencies.

Field Checks

Big name banks have collection criteria that usually begins with sending out a professional representative to the given address to make contact with the debtor. The whole purpose is to make the lender's delinquent customer have an urgent communication that they are behind and let them know the bank is going to begin real efforts in the repossession process. In most cases a door knock is always first used to make contact with the debtor and guide them into bringing payments current.

A field check usually consists of a few visits to the address and attempt to make contact. The bank can get good information to make collection decisions with from your field check.

Vacant houses, new cars in the driveway, if someone has fallen ill or passed away; all real situations that happen and there's no database that anyone has that can provide such information.

Take some pictures of the address and other cars that may be in the driveway. If no one answers the door you may be required to leave a notice on the door with your trap line number or the banks info if they request it, or some other directive of the client. A typical fee for this service is $75.00 to $150.00.

If a debtor tells you that he has filed bankruptcy you cannot make contact with the debtor again. You can ask for a case number and the attorney's name, sometimes you'll get a straight answer and sometimes you'll get the door slammed in your face. But, in either case, you can call the bankruptcy court to verify if that debtor is indeed protected in bankruptcy. If no case is filed you are free to continue to make contact with that debtor.

In a situation where an address is vacant you're not required to skip trace to find a new address, unless of course, this is the deal you made with the client. Don't do it for free though! I do as much free skip tracing as I can do with a few quick affordable and meaningful clicks on some databases. I don't get paid unless I get a car repossessed most of the time so, I want to give myself the best possible chance of getting the collateral picked up.

After the update that the address is vacant you're probably going to get an authorization to repossess for that collateral.

If per chance you knock the debtors door and the debtor says, "Please take this car right now." You should be prepared to take it and make sure that you have an arrangement in place if this should happen.

Yet another thing you may learn on a door knock is that the collateral is in the shop and if the debtor intends to keep the unit or surrender it back to the bank. In this case you may not get an authorization to repossess from a garage right away. But if so, this is called a bail out.

You're bailing the car out of the repair shop; you'll contact the shop, try to negotiate a reduced bill, pay it for your client and get reimbursed in your final bill. The remainder of the recovery stays in line with the repossession protocol you've laid out for your company.

Equipment

When looking to invest in repo truck equipment you'll a popular style of self-loading wrecker. This type of equipment is operated from inside the truck cab and can lift the wheels of a repo off the ground to roll away in less than 15 seconds.

Also referred to as a wheel-lift or a sneaker and popular manufacture names are Dynamic Lift and Illusion. The retracting and moving bars are designed to create a hole where the tires cannot easily come out of.

If the operator is picking up the wrong end of a car, such as picking up a front wheel drive from the rear, the tires will "scream out" as the unit is dragged into a position where the driver can turn around and grab it from the correct end.

Towing and repo equipment can be very different from each manufacturer. Older models can fit into a truck bed or underneath a bumper and newer models completely replace the bed of a truck. Regulations can be put forth in an individual state that restrict light weight trucks and place minimum requirements on the year of the model. Each state enforces its own safety measures for towing and repossession.

As your repo company grows, the need to make your own keys will too. In each VIN number will be a key code. A lien holder may already have this information in the debtors file as this will be a part of the new car package sent to the finance company when a brand new car is sold. Older cars lose that detail after the car is sold on auction.

Vendors that sell key codes are around and market to repo companies, but in most cases you can take your repo order to the maker's parts and service department at a dealership and get at least a key cut that will open the door.

If the car makers service department says they don't do keys any longer it's because of a man posing as a repo man took vehicle information and fake repo orders to a Ford dealership and had keys cut that would open and start over twenty Ford cars, and then stole the cars.

Any future keys are made only for the registered owner of the vehicle and perhaps on a case by case basis. I am sure that if you have a personal contact at a service department you could get special treatment.

You don't necessarily have to have a repo truck to repossess cars. Many smaller finance companies and buy here pay here dealers keep keys and sometimes alarm boxes to the cars they sell. It's not unusual for a repo company to have two man teams in repo trucks so that one person can drive the tow truck and a second person can drive away in the repo.

There may be instances where you can't get a repo truck to a car. Such as one that is parked in a parking garage and a key would help you get the vehicle and get out of the parking garage. The same idea works for gated communities and apartment complexes with live guards. You may not be able to get your tow truck through the guard shack, but you may have another way onto the property and can drive away with the repo.

Sling lifts are usually found on older types of tow trucks and damage bumpers and fenders on today's body styles. When you hear the marketing term, "Damage Free Towing" you can know that the sling lift is not used on the repo trucks.

These tow truck fixtures require a driver to get out of the car and connect chains securing the tires before driving away turning what would only be a few seconds with a wheel lift into minutes and raising the risk of losing the repo to a breach of peace or just confrontation with an angry debtor.

Financed vehicles are a primary investment in a person's life. When it comes to repossessing things that people need, especially a person's primary mode of transportation, which are relied upon by debtors to earn a living and are considered by many as essential objects of self-respect and self worth, disputes and breach of peach can easily become a part of repossession.

You know the messenger is going to get shot, even though I say that figuratively it happens. Repo agents have been killed and permanently disabled by debtors flying high on emotion.

Insurance

Wrongful Repossession

This coverage protects you in the case of a repossession gone wrong. Human error can take a front seat to disaster when a lender fails to notify you of a cancellation in time. When a debtor makes a payment after business hours to a live person at the bank, that debtor may feel safe and leave the car in the driveway.

After hours cancellations that are not faxed immediately could result in an easy repossession although would be a wrongful repossession in the eyes of the debtor. If there is litigation, this coverage protects you as a business owner.

Garage Keepers

This coverage protects collateral while in your care and custody. While on your storage lot or inside your structure such as a mechanic's garage or body shop. Debtors that steal their car back fall into this insurance coverage. This is a good argument for tall fences and well lit storage lots.

Porters

This coverage protects repossessed collateral as it's driven by your employees, as the unit is repossessed and in other instances of being driven by your employees such as to an auction or moving it to another storage lot.

Often repos will be delivered directly to the client or to the auction. Also known as Drive Away Insurance. This could also be a special rider on your personal auto insurance.

Contents Coverage

If valuables disappear or are damaged while in your possession this coverage covers you.

Comprehensive Collision

Accidents that occur while a repo is hooked to your tow truck will be covered by this liability policy. Coverage that far exceeds one million dollars is an industry standard and highly desired by lenders. This policy protects you as a business owner, a tow truck operator and any other party that is involved suffering damages.

Fuel Control

More than a repo truck payment, rising fuel costs have contributed to the most frustrating and difficult costs to maintain in recovery business. Strategy to overcome high fuel bills can be simple skip trace methods and spotters that use fuel efficient cars instead of running blind addresses with gas hogging big trucks. Another idea would to use a zip code zoning method and run accounts by area. In bigger cities such as Chicago one or two areas of the city can covered in a day.

Innovations in technology provide very precise locations. License plate recognition systems use cameras that outfit a car or tow truck snapping the license plate and location information in your own system. License plates also can be run through the system from other companies logging date and time information.

If a license plate hits in a database the fee for purchasing the information can be in the ballpark of $200.00 to $250.00 but if the vehicle is not recovered at the camera's address, the fee is not assessed.

Several companies offer the camera system. These camera systems can be rented or purchased from RDN, Reposystems and MVTrack just to name a few. Ask about refurbished systems to get an affordable start.

A major factor in startup success is to create a list of vehicles with their license plates. Commonly referred to as a "hot sheet" and ideal for spotters to work from because of its easy reference style that keeps a driver from having to fumble through papers to find the deal and verify a license plate or VIN number.

Again, if you're using repo software you'll get this as an instant feature. With just a click you'll get a hot sheet that you can print and keep at your side for easy reference.

REPOSYSTEMS

Discount code for first time subscribers:

Tw2J3

Good Reputation Business

In the insurance business adjusters are required to take 20 or so hours every year in continuing education credit classes. Many online and most are college courses provided at local junior college campuses. Ethics is one of those required classes to be taken every two years. *Even if it's the same exact class with identical content.* The reason is ethics matter and the lack of ethics is the bases of many court actions.

Because many recovery agencies use the word *adjuster* in the company name or call certain employees that work in the field *adjusters*, doesn't mean that they have the same knowledge and ethics base as an insurance adjuster. Yes, it's adjusting per the actual meaning of the word *adjuster* however not the same.

My point truly is that ethical business principles should be important to you and your employees. If it's against the law, don't do it. If it can be misconstrued as an illegal act, don't do it.

If you get into a situation where you would have to take a polygraph to prove something, don't do it. Taking the high road not only protects your investment now, it protects your investment in your future business transactions and your image as a company with a good reputation.

An example of good reputation business is a repo company in Georgia took a skip from Texas and recovered it. This Hummer2 was not in fantastic condition and the battery quickly died. The repo company saw it was a Walmart battery and said they were taking it and exchanging it, they never actually did that for the client.

Being in another state makes the deal a bit harder to stay on top of when phone calls aren't returned. It's common for independent repossessors to run on office staff and on a cell phone as the only means of communication with clients.

Mistake #1 This company didn't do what they said they were going to do and didn't call the lien holder with battery updates.

The lien holder assumed the repo company did what they said they were going to do when in fact, they did not. So, this whole time the client assumed the vehicle was running in pretty good condition.

During this the repo company was asked to get three bids from local businesses to buy the unit since the closest auction was several hundred miles away. The ten days free storage given on the front end of the deal quickly lapsed while the client was waiting for the company to gather bids.

Mistake #2 The repo company didn't advise that while they were taking their sweet time to get three bids for the client that storage fees would begin to be billed on the repossession sitting on their lot, not running due to a dead battery.

Not only was the repo company unable to get good bids on a non running Hummer2, they probably didn't even try. A storage bill of over one thousand dollars was submitted to the client three weeks later. Now the client would have to pay this bill and the recovery bill to get the collateral away from the repo company.

In the midst of all these weeks going by with storage fees compiling the lien holder attempted contact with the repossession agency owner and its employees about bids.

Since the main form of contact was a text message there was a history that showed dates and times to prove either the lack of communication or the answer to the client that the bids had not been collected as of yet. Yes, that's right, avoiding the task and letting storage pile up to bill the lien holder. Crooks.

With no mention whatsoever of how the storage fees were being added daily. This repo company chose to conduct a fleece type maneuver knowing that the bill would have to be paid in full before the unit was released to the auction.

When this situation was addressed all the men that worked together either didn't answer the phone or blamed the high bill on the other owner and said there wasn't anything that could be done about it.

Mistake #3 Hiring me to find out everything I can about who this repo company is and get my client ready for a law suit.

My intentions are to make sure that every finance company that has offices in the state of Georgia knows what this company did to the lien holder by warning them of these fraud business practices. With texting history in hand and a timeline of email exchanges, I intend to at least get someone's attention so they are aware of this scam.

Paperwork

When you get an assignment from your client the first thing you need to do is to confirm that the client has the right to repossess. This is establishing that a security interest exists. A contract between the debtor and client should be available as well as a record with the state where a lien should be clearly listed.

You can ask for the title to be faxed to you and there is another shorter document that is called a buyers order that gives the debtors name, the description of the collateral, amount that is put down on the car, amount that is financed along with a signature of a representative of the lien holder and the signature of the debtor and finance company agreeing to those terms.

You can require that the lender fax over a copy of the title which gives proof that the vehicle is your client's security interests and they have the right to repossess. Repo companies can get an account with the states motor vehicle database to get a confirmation of the paperwork and discover what the license plate is that is on the vehicle. If a debtor switches plates this is where you will find out-directly from the state.

If there is fraud in the paperwork it would be on the side of the debtor giving incorrect information to the lien holder. Fake social security numbers and incomplete addresses are most common. The reference sheet is a collection of names and addresses with phone numbers from the debtor when the car was purchased. I've seen many reference sheets have names and cell phone numbers with no addresses.

The car lot that sells the loan may never check references because they know a finance company is funding the car deal. A reference can be skip traced, but usually not from just a name and a disconnected cell phone number. Make sure your client gets full addresses on those references

The documents that your client provides you should be vehicle information, credit application with signature, reference sheet and pay history. If you have obtained your own credit reporting account from Experian, Equifax or Transunion you need the pay history to prove that you are pulling credit for a debtor that has a delinquency assigned to your company to collect by repossession.

The final piece of paper that you need to have is a Repossession Order. The standard order is shown in figure 1.

MY REPO COMPANY
123 Any St.
Los Angeles, CA 90001

REPO ORDER

Debtor Info:
JOSE A. GARCIA
12345 HIDE OUT AVE.
LOS ANGELES, CA

DRIVERS LIC: 0012345678
D.O.B. 05/16/1991

Vehicle Info:
2G1WT55K688888899
2007 CHEVROLET IMPALA
SEDAN 4-DR
License plate: CT3Z309

Lien Holder:
USA AUTO FINANCE
(555) 567-7777

Hold Harmless:
This is your authorization to act as our agents to collect or repossess the above mentioned collateral. We agree to indemnify and hold harmless from and against any and all claims, damages, losses and actions, including reasonable attorney fees, resulting from and arising out of your efforts to collect and/ or repossess claims, except however such as may be caused by or arise out of the negligence or unauthorized act on the part of you, your company, it's officers, employees or it's agents.

X_____
Authorized Signature

Fig 1

If the police are called out by the debtor you must have the correct paper work to prove that you aren't just stealing a car. In many towns the police require a repo company to check-in with them either in person or by phone announcing that you're repossessing a vehicle and show authorizing paperwork.

For many reasons, obviously the main one being that if a debtor calls the police they already know why you're there and know there's not a real car theft in progress. As well as protecting you in the event of a act of hindering or other violent reaction by the debtor to your action of recovering their vehicle.

Police are (in most states) not allowed to get involved with a repossession in progress unless there is a claim of a breach of the peace. That means that the debtor claims you went into a locked garage, trespassed, cause property damage of some other sort or PHYSICAL force during the attempt to repossess.

I've heard of police pulling over a repo truck with a unit on the hook that was just repossessed and made the driver give the car back to the debtor because the repo was not checked in with the local police department beforehand. It pays to call ahead and ask when going to a town or parish that you've never worked in before.

After a client assigns an account to your repo company, it's common to get a daily call asking for updates. Some of the online data retrieval systems such as Reposystems.com (don't forget promo code to get discounts on new subscriptions: **Tw2J3)** have a built in service that automatically sends updates to the client via email or fax.

These systems are extremely convenient and even have features that allow updates to be added to an account via text message. Creating the good habit of sending a text when you are at an account's address will help you stay on top of your accounts. Trust me, it's easy to lose track and forget things that can help you in the future. Especially when a volume of work starts rolling in.

The only downfall to having automatic updates is that any information placed into the update section of the system on each account would be sent to the client. Create a positive routine where you can send an email or fax to your client outside the updating feature.

You could be hurt by allowing the client to know about phone number and new address information. I consider this type of update to be secret and confidential. *Maybe even referred to as a trade secret.*

To prevent this from happening, don't enter your clients email or fax number into the client contact on the system so that you don't lose control over the new information you worked to discover. That client should not get those notes in any updates.

I say don't enter it in a client's fax and email all because there is a selection that you can choose to turn on or off this feature and if the info isn't there to begin with it can't accidentally end up being sent to your client if someone else changes the settings. In this business, information is money just as the time that you spend gathering the info that gets your pay day earned.

I absolutely know to be true that a lien holder looking at paying you a big bill will take one tiny piece of information and turn that into a situation where the collateral gets repossessed by another company or closed in some other manner.

I never give out debtor contact information or details of the continuing investigation directly to the client because double assigning happens regularly and you have no recourse if you're cheated out of a deal. Keep it covert.

After the repossession is complete and you've picked up the collateral there are some paperwork steps that could represent your top notch service. The first one is pictures of the repo that covers the interior, odometer and other gages (even if you don't have a key, take a picture) and seats. The front and back from both left and right angles.

Photos of every side of the vehicle, front, back, drivers and passengers side. Take extra pictures focusing on body damage of the repo if there is any. The condition report is much like the report that a car rental service does when a rental is checked in. It gives blank fields for the condition of the paint, tires and all glass.

Most repo system software has a built in condition report that has boxes to tick for features of the unit and what condition it was at the time of recovery. Some condition reports are not in depth while others are.

If a unit goes to auction it will be appraised and sometimes repaired so that it'll sell for more money. If you also have a auto repair crew you could offer this service to your client at competitive rates to get this business and offer more of a turn-key package to your clients.

Vehicle Condition Report

Customer Name _____ Vehicle:
Address _____ Year _____ Make _____
Phone # _____ Model _____ Color _____
Dealer Name _____ Style _____ Body _____
Address _____ VIN _____
Phone _____ License # _____ Mileage _____

CHECK OPTIONS INCLUDED ON VEHICLE				
☐ ABS 4 Wheel	☐ Bedliner	☐ Cruise Control	☐ Moon or Sun Roof	☐ Power Windows
☐ Air Cond.	☐ Camper Shell	☐ Custom Bumper	☐ Power Door Locks	☐ Roof Rack
☐ AM-FM Radio	☐ C.D.	☐ Leather Interior	☐ Power Seats	☐ Running Boards
☐ Auto. Trans.	☐ C.D. Changer	☐ Luxury/Sport Pkg.	☐ Power Steering	☐ Rear Sliding Window
☐ Wide Tires	☐ Sport Wheels	☐ Stereo	☐ Tilt Wheel	☐ Tow Package

CONDITION OF VEHICLE

Indicate any damage to the vehicle in the space provided using your own words or the following legend. If None write None

| H – Hairline Scratch | PT – Pitted | T – Torn | B – Bent | GC – Glass Cracked | M – Missing |
| SM – Smashed | R – Rusty | CR – Creased | S – Scratched | ST – Stained | BR – Broken | D – Dented |

FRONT
1. _____
2. _____
3. _____
4. _____
5. _____

BACK
6. _____
7. _____
8. _____
9. _____
10. _____

DRIVER'S SIDE

PASSENGER'S SIDE

| 11. | 12. | 13. | 17. | 18. | 19. |
| 14. | 15. | 16. | 20. | 21. | |

INTERIOR					
☐ CLEAN	☐ AVERAGE			☐ DIRTY	
	Good	Worn	Burns	Rips	Stain
Front Carpet	☐	☐	☐	☐	☐
Rear Carpet	☐	☐	☐	☐	☐
Front Seat	☐	☐	☐	☐	☐
Rear Seat	☐	☐	☐	☐	☐
Headliner	☐	☐	☐	☐	☐
Door Panels	☐	☐	☐	☐	☐
Dash	☐ Dent	☐ Crack		☐ Holes	

MECHANICAL				
Engine	☐ Smooth	☐ Rough	☐ Knock	
Trans / Clutch	☐ Seems OK	☐ Slips		
Air	☐ Blows Hot			
Brakes	☐ Seems OK	☐ Difficult		
Exhaust	☐ Seems OK	☐ Needs Replacement		
Power Malfunction	☐ Windows	☐ Seats	☐ Locks	☐ Roof
Sound Equip.	☐ Inoperative			

Tires	Right Front	Left Front	Right Rear	Left Rear	Spare
Good					☐ Missing
Fair					☐ Included
Poor					

Fig. 2

Associations

Recovery associations for the repossession industry create a high standard for compliance with federal and state laws. Associations give your company credibility and protection offering members additional insurance coverage in the event that your client is sued for an alleged action by your company.

Marketing is a part of the associations function as they reach out to mainstream lenders nationwide and provide lenders with your contact information on their websites and in printed publications.

Most associations host an annual national convention where lenders, members and vendors meet and learn about new innovations and technology introduced to the profession.

Time Finance Adjusters-has online directory of members and hardcover book available to anyone upon request. Can be located on the web at
http://www.timefinanceadjusters.com

Allied Finance Adjusters-
http://www.alliedfinanceadjusters.com

C.A.R.S.-A national certification program that is accepted by the state of Florida for repossession licensure and is a home study with online testing. Available through http://www.riscus.com/

Laws

Every state has a different statute regarding the recovery of secured collateral. There are laws that say the debtor is committing a felony if the unit isn't surrendered upon demand and there are other laws that say a car can't be repossessed without a court order. Court cases both civil and criminal have shaped each state's legislature on enforcing a security interest.

A breach of peace is a standard "out" for a debtor to claim, even if there isn't an altercation. Accusations of repo men grabbing keys out of a debtor's hand, pulling a debtor out of car or other physical contact would convince a police officer to not allow the repo to be taken from the debtor and possibly get a repo man arrested with his tow truck impounded.

Service Members Civil Relief Act protects military from evictions and secured collateral repossessions. If a vehicle is repossessed from an enlisted and active duty service member the lien holder may have to pay back to the debtor any equity from the sale of the car and it is written that the entire payments for the car may have to be returned to the debtor.

This also covers all secured collateral purchased before the debtor enlists. Do this due diligence to verify that the debtor is not protected by this act at the time of repossession.

The only protection that a lien holder has is to have the debtor sign a waiver specifically detailing that the debtor waives all rights under the Service Members Civil Relief act and stating the lien holder has the right to repossess for non-payment and no insurance coverage or any other failure to perform according the contract between the debtor and lien holder.

In an event that the law is changed and disallows a debtor from waiving his rights having the form signed at a time when the right can be waived would be considered covered and the collateral would be good to be repossessed. Regardless of how this law is worded at the time of signing the waiver or at the time of assignment for repossession consulting with an attorney would be advisable.

The Service Members Civil Relief Act says that the waiver must be in at least 12 point font size (which means not fine print) and must be on a separate sheet of paper aside from the contract. Before collateral is sequestrated in a court of law the person must be verified as not being a service member and that proof is attached to the original petition filed with the court.

Font Size Example
This sentence is 12 point font size.
This sentence is 11 point font size.
This sentence is 10 point font size.

One thing you can rely on, if it's against the law for a citizen to do, it's also against the law for a repo man to do. Having an authorization to repossess does give you the right to legally steal a car, but how you get it matters.

Trespassing is a common accusation and a typical complaint not to mention the usual basis for a lawsuit in civil court. I've peeked into many garage door windows and even lifted the door half an inch or so to see if there was a vehicle sitting in the garage but actually opening the door could put a repo man in hot water.

A pretext would be to carry a dog leash in your hand so that you have an excuse of looking for your dog when looking in a garage or a backyard.

Sometimes a garage has a separate door on the side so that a person can enter without opening the garage doors. You could try knocking on that door first before trying the handle to see if you can peek inside the garage. Just make sure your actions are quick so that if someone sees you it looks completely innocent.

When there is a civil remedy to a criminal action, that civil remedy must be taken first. Attempts to get the debtor to pay current, certified letters to cure, repossession attempts and finally a civil judgment and sequestration filing for the vehicle.

Collateral can still be out for repossession with your company while the sequestration hearings are scheduled. Sequestration hearing orders and final orders in most states can only be served by a local constable, but not every debtor is going to know this.

Also when you get the final writ of sequestration have certified copies with the tow trucks rolling so that if it's spotted the police can actually be called and turned over to you without a struggle.

Need to verify a handwritten VIN? Carfax.com will autocorrect a VIN and give make & model with color too!

Threatening to "go legal" by a lien holder are followed by attempts to make contact by a stranger will make the debtor think that they are being served. It could have more of a negative result when you are trying to get a car picked up. Negotiations at this time would be telling the debtor if they would give up the car peacefully then they would not have to go to court, could really work to your advantage.

Hindering a Secured Creditor laws are in all fifty states and they all say about the same thing. This law makes it a violation to possess secured collateral if the car has not been paid for and the lien holder has made a documented demand for the vehicle.

This demand could come in the form of a phone call, mail, certified letters (demand to cure letters) and attempting to make personal contact with a repossession agent. After the demand has been made to return the vehicle and the debtor failed to return the collateral, then a felony crime is committed.

Also, the misconception by a debtor is that they have the legal right to possess a vehicle just because their name is on the title. This couldn't be further from the truth. Obviously this is why we have job security. People get behind and make it hard for the lien holder to adjust the losses by taking back the collateral and liquidating it.

The lien holder and debtor are in a legally binding contract and if the debtor fails to keep their end of the contract, the contract is breached and terminated. The debtor is only allowed to drive the car while the contract is paid out. The debtor doesn't have full legal rights to any collateral until the final and last payment is made.

Other points of the Hindering a Secured Creditor statutes in most states are taking the collateral outside the state without written permission from the line holder, moving without giving notice, encumbering collateral by abandoning it in the shop with repair work and also destroying it to hide it.

Concealing it as in giving it away to someone else or hiding it in a garage. This law also provides a way to charge a person with a felony if the collateral is deliberately reduced in value. This could be if the motor was removed or the car stripped. Also the value of the vehicle measures the severity of punishment. The more the car is worth, the more the fine and minimum jail time sentenced.

DTPA and Pretexting

The Deceptive Trade Practices Act and pretexting are important issues to a repo man. This act defines what deception is in the act of gaining personal information from someone for personal gain. Pretexting to do a job is not normally defined as a deception for personal gain.

You're not going to get some bank account information and drain the account by fraudulent means. You're simply putting a process in motion that could give some good details as to where a person would be at a certain time so that you can get that person face to face or uneventfully get a unit repossessed.

The normal hold harmless form that you get when you are assigned a repo says that you can't be sued by the assignor for any normal lawful action taken to repossess their car. But, it usually plainly says that you are not held harmless from any malicious act or an act that is illegal.

Pretexting is a practice used to create a circumstance where a target person would innocently give up information. It could be as simple as calling as a lost deliveryman or offering a free pizza in exchange for a survey on the quality of the pizza.

There is an underlying truth to using the law to scare debtors into giving up a repo without argument. Most people don't want problems with the law. Property owners don't want to have lien put on their property in the event they lose a judgment, wages garnished or even want to appear in court with the threat of being served.

Just remember that impersonation of a government employee is a felony just like hiding the car from the lien holder is. The last thing any repo man wants is to get a reputation for getting their clients into hot water with the law or the subject of a civil suit brought by the debtor. And, if your actions bring a suit to your clients, you can expect to be sued as well.

Now that you know the basic boundaries of pretexting, you'll know not to brag about how you use a pretext or even give away any pretexting secrets to *anyone* else. These are unadvertised secrets that are meant to be kept. That includes your clients as well as any new employees that may not be with your company for long. Your pretexts are part of your repo trade secrets.

I've a compilation of pretexts in a book called The Pretext Play Book and in it are contributions of over 100 private investigators, repo men, skip tracers, process servers and bounty hunters that know the "pretexting" ropes. If you know other repo men ask advice on the topic and what works best for uncovering information that will get the repo done. There are links to this and other investigative books in the recommended reading chapter of this book.

Personal Property

Personal property inside a repo should only be released to the registered owner on the title. You are not required by law to release it to anyone else. I made it a common practice to tell the debtor that I'll only release personal property in exchange for the keys to the unit.

The longest that you're required to hold personal property for someone to pick up is thirty days, however, this can vary from state to state as well as county or city. After that, you can discard, donate or reuse anything inside.

Personal property specifically is not anything that is bolted down. Meaning stereo equipment, speakers, CD players, DVD players, amps or display screens are a permanent part of the vehicle. I think it's a better practice to remove all of the personal property and hand it to the debtor inside the office than allow the debtor inside a repo to get their own things.

I've seen many a debtor whip a screw driver out and start removing bolted down items. Regardless of if upgraded after the car was purchased or not, when the car was picked up the opportunity to remove those items has been lost.

On the flip side a common accusation for a debtor to make is that their personal property that was inside the car is missing. Perfume, cell phones, cameras, and cash just to name a few have been on the list of things missing from a repo. I'll never understand why people leave expensive items inside a vehicle that is out for repo, but it does happen.

Missing items may not follow under the terms of your hold harmless but there should be a company policy in place to keep other employees from being tempted to take things out of a repo at will. There also should be a sign in your office where debtors wait to retrieve their personal property stating that you are not responsible for items missing from inside a repossessed vehicle.

Having the debtor sign a form stating that they received all their personal property at the time of surrendering the key would be an ideal situation. You could create a form where the debtor waives the ten day waiting period for the lien holder to sell the car combined with a personal property release form.

Charging fee's to collect and store personal property is fine as long as it's legal. If your state says you can't charge that type of fee then you have to take a pass on this one but the usual fee to the debtor is between $50.00 and $150.00.

Releasing Collateral

There are four situations where collateral is released. First, a person from the lien holder comes to pick up the vehicle from you directly or you deliver it directly to the lien holder and drop it off on their property. Second, you release it to a transportation company. And third, you release the repo back to the debtor. Lastly you'll deliver to auction or the auction will pick up from you.

Releasing the vehicle back to the debtor is called a replevin. Releasing the repo to anyone else is just simply releasing it. In any situation, the paper work that you need is a signed release from and authorized person with the lien holder giving you an exact direction of what to do with the unit.

Even if you only get a handwritten letter directing you to release the unit to another party, get that letter. It can be proven by the date and time stamp on the fax if nothing else.

Another iffy part of releasing collateral is getting paid. It should be your company policy to not release any collateral to anyone until the repo fee has been paid. Transportation companies and auto auctions will have an account with a lien holder and will write you a check when you release the collateral. If you're afraid of getting a check bounced on you then only take cash. Note lots deal in cash and most likely will pay you cash. In any case, you can ask for it.

A very good reason why this is an issue is that checks bounce and collateral is liquidated making a second repossession and repo lien a slim chance to complete. If there's no collateral to repossess for no payment of repo fees then all you can do is collect and file a lawsuit.

The transportation company, the lien holder and the debtor all should get you paid before you release the repo into anyone's possession. An angle to that iffy part is when you deliver a repo to a lien holder; don't disconnect the car from your repo truck until you get paid.

Let the collateral sit on your hook and if you get the gates closed on you and you're getting a refusal to pay, call the local law enforcement. You know I'm telling you this because many note lot dealers are also used car salesmen and I've seen so much fraud it's absolutely worth discussing.

Here in Los Angeles there was a tote-your-note lot that got into me for 12 repo deals. I waited for many months for payment and always got a promise to pay with new work. I had keys to the gate at the car lot and would just drop the repo off on the way home.

I was thinking that it was saving me time and gas by avoiding a second trip to drop off and get paid. Finally, I had enough of the run around. I arranged for me and six other local repo trucks to hit this car lot and pick up what cars that were still on the lot that I had orders for and had remaining unpaid invoices and hold those units on a storage lot.

Nine of the twelve cars were on the lot and when the entire bill was settled I got my repo fee, a second repo fee and a delivery charge to transport all the cars back. The dealership owner walked into my office with over $14,000.00 in cash the next day.

I received an humbling apology and after fiasco I never take the car off the hook until I get paid first. My company policy continued to evolve because I needed more safeguards in place to protect me and my livelihood. You'll find out that will be the way you'll want to conduct business too.

Why Operation Repo is Bad

When this outrageous repo show came on the air I watched the first few episodes and instantly knew it was garbage. The entire show was marketed to be unrehearsed and "live" with the style of inner circle arguments and assaulting altercations between the debtor and repo man.

Every single show has a written script with actors. Violent acts between the debtor and repossessor on the street are on the rise because of Lizard Lick, South Beach Tow and Operation Repo style shows.

And every single show has its characters in a flagrant violation of the law. You can't go on one someone's property and take a car out of a garage, you cannot walk into a trailer and take ATV's out of the trailer, and you can't remove collateral that the debtor is occupying such as on the back of an ATV, motorcycle or a boat. You absolutely are not allowed to pull someone out of a vehicle.

If you touch the debtor and forcefully remove (or knock them clean off the collateral like acted out on the repo shows) you're committing bodily assault and breaching the peace. Any show that glamorizes repossessions is doing it for ratings.

They're not doing it to show you the right way to repo collateral. Every person on the show is a paid actor performing a script even if they also do work in the repo industry in real life.

I think there are about a million excellent Youtube videos that repo men make to show the right way to repo collateral. When you start watching them you'll get lost in those videos because there are so many good ones.

Gotbad is a YouTube handle of a repo man that has been doing repossessions for many years and he talks through his videos explaining the entire situation from beginning to end. The comments on his videos are from many people just like you, learning the business. Gotbad takes the time to answer questions.

Some people watch stupid repo shows and think that starting a fight with a repo man will help them keep their car. I don't know how many people on Operation Repo actually went to jail for some of the stunts they pull, but it's a scripted show. So, I guess no one ever really goes to jail. But they do in real life!

Stages of a Repo

Here is a checklist of action to take from getting the repo assignment to finishing up the deal with getting paid.

-Receive assignment.

-Check for hold harmless, references, credit application and vehicle info.

-Check VIN for lien, make sure lien holder still has right to repossess. (Mechanic liens won't' have this, must have unpaid invoice with VIN or plate number and description of car)

-Place repo order and paperwork in the truck for verification of VIN and quick reference if needed by police department.

-Check the Google Map and Mapquest views of the address where you're going to. Look to see if anyone parks cars in the backyard or if the house even has a garage. Google Street View and Mapquest can do this free.

-Check with police department to know if an in person check in or phone in check in is needed before attempt to repo.

-Run given address without making contact at least six times, various times of the day.

-Knock door and make contact asking for collateral.

-If vacant, advise client of updates and ask for current address information.

-Send certified mail to address if vacant to see if forwarded.

-Talk to neighbors.

-Get authorization for your own skip trace efforts, if charging an additional fee for skip tracing.

-Run through databases.

-Attempt to make contact with all references.

-Skip trace references

-Leave cards on door of address that you know is good for debtor, if no answer.

-When repossessed call into local police department and get control number.

-Take repo to secured storage lot.

-Search for guns and drugs, report those to the local police department.

-Get paid!

Google Street View is AWESOME! But the actual film is shot months or even years before.

Getting the Repo vs. Getting the Key

It's happens time and time again. I find my repo, I get the car blocked in or I get my tow truck hooked up and I am so confident that I knock the door and ask for the key. Here's why asking for a key is a bad thing: it gives a debtor an opportunity to stop the repo.

Some people watch stupid shows like Operation Repo and think that starting a fight with a repo man will help them keep their car. I don't know how many people on Operation Repo actually went to "fake repo show jail" for some of the stunts they pull, but it's a scripted show. So, I guess no one ever really goes to jail.

I located a Porche in Los Angeles this past year and the debtor was an attorney. Tracking down all of this guy's relatives was fairly easy. The entire family was in the restaurant supply business and they were all property owners. The car appeared at the sisters house and I blocked it and and knocked on the door to get the key.

Because the car was over twelve thousand dollars past due I never believed that there would ever be any argument over the car. The sister answered the door and came outside with the keys and started getting her things out.

> Hate to be so mean! When a debtor dodges me for many months I leave a business card right where the car was towed from.

When she went inside to get keys to Porsche she either called or texted her brother, the debtor. What we didn't know was her brother gave her the car and she was really mad about us showing up to take it from her with no warning. She believed that the title was clear and the car was paid off.

The debtor showed up and called the police. The debtor had a *photograph* of a clear title on his cell phone and showed the police the picture trying to say that there was no lien on it.

I called the afterhours contact for the lien holder and got that person to speak to the police officer wanting to be able to prove without a shadow of a doubt that there is a good and current lien on the car and it was a good repo. The officer verified there was a lien on it, had a repo order with an original signature on it and still allowed the debtor to haul the car away on a flat bed.

The end reason was because the debtor claimed we breached the peace by jerking the keys out of the sister's hand which was a complete and total lie.

If this had been a police department that required a repossessor check in before the repo was done, the police would already know that we had the correct paperwork and verified that the lien was correctly done and the lien holder did in fact have the right to repossess. I did eventually find the Porsche and get it picked up and I never made contact with anyone to get a key either!

Dashboard Cams

In Russia the police take a very long time to come to the scene of auto accidents and so people use dashboard cameras to prove what actually happened. Affordable dash cam's can be found on eBay that include everything you need including the memory card to record on.

These are full color cameras with sound and infrared night vision. These little cameras even come with suction cup mounts so that they can be attached to any window (or all windows) in your truck.

Some cameras are more expensive with looping recording, meaning when the card is full it records over the oldest recording (usually stored in 110 second segments). Other camera's that are in the twenty dollar range don't have this feature and you'll have to have extra memory cards with no files on them to continue to record.

To be able to use an old card I've to erase all the memory files by connecting it into my computer. The non-looping kind would be excellent if you have a 128 gig card in the camera. Then you wouldn't lose recordings and have them to go back to for a while, at least until you choose the right time to erase the data and use it again.

The number one best reason to use dashboard camera's is so that you can prove that you didn't do anything wrong. I've had debtors throw themselves into the repo, their babies and even their dogs.

Debtors have jumped in the repo and drive it off my rig, and even debtors throw themselves onto the ground under the wheels of the repo and claim that I deliberately ran over them. All disproven because I've used a camera in the front and back of my trucks for the past ten years.

In early summertime 2013 two women attempting to repossess a vehicle at a carwash were run over by the debtor. One repo woman was standing behind the unit and her partner was standing inside the open driver side door speaking to the debtor behind the wheel.

The debtors name is Rakia Lewis and she is facing two counts of attempted manslaughter in Jennings, Louisiana. Just a few days later in Vacaville, California another debtor hit a repo man while fleeing in the collateral.

Jessie Williams, 28, confronted the repo man knocking him down as he got into the unit to drive away, but drove over the repossession agent during his escape. Jessie Williams was later found and charged with assault with a deadly weapon. This is just a very small sampling of insane behavior by debtors.

GPS

Just like a GPS locating device embedded on the iPhone, GPS devices work to provide a location by satellite pinging. There are several different applications for a GPS to work for a repo man. The legality of using GPS devices are entirely a different subject which varies from state to state. Reasons for using GPS devices and the main idea of using a GPS in most repo maneuvers are illegal.

In states where a GPS locating device is illegal to place on collateral by a lien holder, it's also illegal for the mechanic to place (by hardwiring) the device as well as the repo man to remotely access the device to get a location from it for the purpose of repossession.

The language that defines how a GPS locating device in legislature gives a lien holder options for a waiver. This waiver cannot be in small print and it must be on a separate piece of paper. Meaning no fine print is allowed (font size under 12) and certainly not any fine print on a contract for a buyer to easily misconstrue for terms on repayment of the loan.

This procedure was created to identify this action to the debtor and allow them to legally acknowledge that there's a location tracking device and there is no reasonable expectation to privacy by the installation of the device.

Other GPS locating devices are sold that can be attached to the undercarriage of the vehicle by a magnet. One name brand that Radio Shack sells is called Zoombak. It does what a repo man needs with a few added perks.

The device sends a text message to your cell phone to notify you when the device has moved several feet and can be programmed to update you with address information in specified time intervals. This is referred to on most GPS programs as a geo-fence. If you need to know when a blocked-in car moves at least a few feet, or a car blocking in your repo leaves, then this handy device is the best medicine.

Using this type of GPS is better than putting a spotter down the street which in turn could scare the debtor into hiding. These are not disposable devices so I recommend that you activate and maintain your subscription with a prepaid credit card and a burner cell phone so that you can't be traced to a device that's accidentally discovered.

OnStar is a great invention that gives peace of mind to drivers. OnStar is that the service will not under any circumstances give out location information of the vehicle to anyone. It doesn't matter if the lien holder or the actual owner of the vehicle calls OnStar with a request.

The only entity that can call OnStar to get a real time location is the person that owns the OnStar subscription. If there is a theft report on the vehicle police then OnStar will release the location however, there could be restrictions about who the location information is released to.

Shut-off devices work in a vehicle's electrical system to completely shut down the ignition and starter making a debtor call to the finance company. Usually when a debtor makes a payment the device can be turned back on and the debtor can start the vehicle again.

Shut-off devices also provide GPS locating. The one downfall of this type of control over the collateral and debtor are once the vehicle has been shut off by the lien holder they have been removed by the debtor making tracking the vehicle's whereabouts impossible.

The downside of GPS units installed by the client is that you could use up a lot of time and gas chasing addresses that the client calls you with. The very best way to get a GPS car repossess is to have your own control over pinging the GPS.

That way you don't have to drop what you are doing and run over to a shopping center to have the car on the move again by the time you actually get there.

Here's a quick explanation of how you can make your own GPS tracking device out of a cheap Android smart phone and an external device battery charger.

Get your phone set up on an unlimited plan, install parental phone tracking software such as the free phonetracker.com or txtwatcher.com, or both! I use both. Attach the fully charged phone to the fully charged backup battery using appropriate cords and connectors.

The battery backup should charge the phone without having to be turned on or any button pressed, but when power is able to flow into the phone on a depleted cell that it will naturally.

Turn off all the sound and vibration the Android device. Fully charge the phone, turn all the screens dark and on the lowest power settings available. This means the phone screen goes black after a few seconds and won't remain lighted.

Both of these free tracking programs will get a location of the phone if the power is on. One of them will only update when the phone is texted. Having both in case of some malfunction is wise. If the hard drive on the phone will function with a third tracking software, do that as well.

Making sure that everything works as you wish put the devices connected by the phone's cable into a sandwich zip bag and then into another. Create a soft black dark package by wrapping it or using a neoprene case.

Getting creative here to hide the potentially visually shocking tracking unit would be good, finding "cases" for car parts to fabricate the entire unit into and bolt on 20 to 60 lb magnets is ideal. Plastic is better as metal can diminish the signal on the cell phone.

Test placement on various types of vehicles when you get all this done, use it, drive around with it and work out the issues that prevent the device from functioning while taking note of the time that you have for the phone to stay powered on and then you have one perfect GPS low cost device.

Skip Trace

When you request paperwork from your client you can ask for any other piece of paper that the client thinks will help you get their car picked up. Buy here pay here dealers sometimes will even write down the license plate of a different car the debtor comes to make a payment arrives in.

Tracing license plates and phone numbers from caller I.D. can give you a new leads where there's no other avenue to go. Collection attempt notes that tell what days phone calls were made and to whom can be of great help.

Returned mail, disconnected phone numbers and details from past conversations let you know if new phone numbers are actually old phone numbers so that you don't waste your time and effort on dead ends and also gives you a time stamp of sorts for undated database records with that same information.

Skip tracing can be as easy. Having some general knowledge of how to hunt a skipped repossession in your area using online free city, county and state databases can help you get repossessions that no other repo company can.

These sites are most likely to be free and give traffic ticket court dates, red light camera tickets, evictions, criminal charges and convictions, if the debtor is out on bond and who the bonding company is, family court filings such as divorce or child support are all things that typically happen in everyday life. If not directly to your debtor, then maybe to someone that the debtor was living with.

If there was an eviction filed with the courts, then maybe the skip put a change of address in with the post office or moved in with a relative. Sometimes when a debtor moves they feel like they can't be found at the new address and skip on making their car payments.

Sending a simple letter with "Address Service Requested" under the return address can net you the forwarding address. Hopefully it's to a residence where the debtor really lives and stays. At the very least it would be to a family member's home or post office box where your mail will be received and you'll get a phone call in return.

Having a licensed PI on staff for a repo company can be helpful when getting information from apartment complex employees, old or current employers or speaking to neighbors.

Additional licenses that provide a photo ID card could prove useful such as a state approved process server. Having these types of licenses can be a instant trust factor for many people that need to make sure you are on the up and up about asking for location information, and can be trusted to

Skip tracing is so much more than just calling someone and asking where the debtor is. Valerie McGilvrey wrote a great book about how she finds debtors for repossessions. She has been skip tracing and cyber tracking debtors for many years and I am very fond of the way she approaches skip tracing not to mention she is first go to person for credit reports.

The name of her book is Skip Trace Secrets Dirty little tricks skip tracers use... If a database search doesn't give fresh address and phone information for your debtor then you have to employ some skip trace secrets that are explained in this book. The site you can read more is LearnSkipTracing.com

Repossession work is a very nocturnal job. Traditionally people work during the day and just aren't around for you to repossess their car. This is why knocking the neighbor's doors can be very useful. One of the most productive questions to ask is when the debtor is usually home.

Other questions can be about what color and what kind of automobiles are in the driveway when someone is home. It's not impossible that your debtor no longer lives there or has given the car away to someone else.

Asking questions simple questions to neighbors can get you closer to the truth, if not closer to your repo. Just know that it's a violation of the FDCPA for you to give actual debt information to anyone but the debtor and the debtor's spouse.

A mom, sister or boyfriend may ask how far they are behind, but you can't give that information. A good response that keeps you in the clear is that you just don't know and the debtor can call the lien holder and get the past due amount directly from them. You are just assigned the account to get the vehicle picked up.

The FDCPA does allow you to ask anyone about the location of the debtor, so you can do this with a clear conscience and don't have any restrictions on who you ask location information to.

Finder's fees are another great tool to use in repossessions. If you find a neighbor could have useful information but would be holding back, or you want to offer a reward to the neighbor for calling you when your repo is sitting in the driveway, offering a cash payment could be just the ticket. It's quite often that a client will authorize a finder's fee to be paid out on the account. All you have to do is ask.

Cell phone forensics is at the center of wonder for me and how it advances, how the average person has no regard for privacy because if the convenience of using a phone to control their entire life. A larger part of communication today is text messaging. In a situation where a person won't answer a strange phone call the confidence in text messaging is high.

Huge companies use text alerts to link an account holder with goods and services giving people a reason to pay attention to certain types of texts or simply be bothered with text messages delivered to their phones.

True cell phone pinging with an outside company would be a dream come true for many professions that hunt for people. Simple versions of this technology exist and although now in this advanced age of the internet and the need for being connected is a standard priority, we believe that this service will be on the rise in the near future.

A fantastic database to all repossessors to have is skipsmasher.com and they have a cell phone ping service that is a no hit fee in addition to a very strong cell phone reverse database.

Another is 3shark.com which is cell phone pinging similar to Skipsmasher but claims to use different technology and was created by programmers for law enforcement to utilize as an answer to highly over priced cell phone tracking systems such as the Harris Stingray.

Impersonating a Police Officer

Competition is high among repo companies. So high in fact that the way you work and reputation to get cars picked up as quickly as possible is what keeps you knee deep in repo orders. Some of my own competition has been caught using pretexts that are completely below the belt.

Of course, these pretexts are made to scare people into submission and turn over the collateral on the first attempt of making contact. Yet they are in violation of the law on city, state and federal levels. I would not be willing to lay down my future for just one repo gone badly.

The man I am going to talk about today is Wayne Waters. He is a tall black man that dresses in black tactical pants and a black shirt wearing a gun in a holster and a very authentic badge around his neck.

His wrinkle was to tell debtors that he is a constable and that he was there to pick up the car with a court order. Wayne got just about every car he went after and the clients loved him. But he made mistakes that made me want to check him out.

First I got him to fax me all his insurance, price schedules and other documents that he was sending to my clients. And, he did, fax me very nice paperwork without any proof of insurance. His cover sheet had a badge on the background and he claimed to be a private investigator. That was easy enough to disprove.

I checked with the California board that governs private investigators and he has never had a license. I also found that he was on probation for a domestic violence case that would also make it a felony to carry a firearm. He also was under a protective order making it an even greater felony because the nature of the crime was domestic violence.

I called three different agencies to report his activities and finally got one agency's department for major offenders to take me seriously. I explained to the local city police that all they had to do was go to a car lot that they had a relationship with and call him from there, asking him to come over and meet with them about getting repo assignments. I believed that the official looking outfit that he wore was a standard law enforcement uniform that got him clients and got cars from debtors.

He was a narcissist and wouldn't dream of walking into a first meeting with a client without his gun and dressed like our local constables.

And he did, and he was arrested for impersonating a private investigator and later charged with impersonating a police officer, carrying a weapon while on probation and while under a protective order. Let's just say this jerk finally got some much deserved justice behind bars.

Every repo company has a different way that they work. Skip tracers are known to use pretexting in every skip trace investigation that's at a dead end with no place to turn. I've heard of calling the relatives as a process server with papers to serve the debtor.

Doing this will let you have a way of contacting the debtors family and references without mentioning the debt at all. Since it's a crime to evade service and to help someone evade as well; this is a very realistic pretext that can get you a return phone call on your trap line. But this move is also a very thin line to cross.

In most states it's illegal to serve someone papers and say they are not court papers just to get them to take the papers and the vice versa, serving someone papers that are not court papers, and saying to them that they are court papers.

So, if you tell someone that they need to meet with a constable to receive some court summons so that a judge can order them to surrender a vehicle and a judgment can be entered against them, you might find someone who is willing to just turn over the vehicle without having to go to court.

Trap Line

This is a special phone line that takes the block off of phone calls made with a privacy block preventing you from seeing the phone number on your caller ID. Some companies that provide this service are Ureach.com and Trapcall.com, the later being my personal favorite simply because people recognize a local cell phone number and don't feel compromised by calling it back.

A toll free phone number is protected by a federal telecommunications statute that says because you pay for the usage on incoming calls that caller I.D. cannot be blocked.

Even if someone blocks or restricts their phone number you'll be able to see the actual phone number from the call list on your account page. If you find an affordable toll number it will do this for you, just get the free trial and test the number before you buy the service.

Take the toll-free phone number you are about to get for your account and Google that before you add it to your account. Only get a toll free number that is completely unattached.

For an example, if a web site has phone complaints connected to that phone number you don't want it. If the number gives no results on a Google or Bing search then you're getting a fresh phone number that has no reputation or connection to anther collection agency or corporation.

Stay away from repetitive numbers and 800 numbers due to the high chance that they were connected to a big business before released. This could save you a small bundle in minute usage fees.

A return phone call has a better chance of happening if it's a cell phone number, even if the caller blocks their phone number. The trap service unblocks the number and will text you the caller ID name and address if the information is available. Trapcall.com starts at $5.00 a month.

Trap lines are best used with cards left on doors. Every time you go to an address and don't get an answer to your knock, leave a card on the door. The best trap line service that exists that will work with your own cell phone is Trapcall.com and using a known local cell phone number for a trap line does produce results. You'll find that people are more inclined to call a cell phone number than they are a toll free or office number.

If the person calling blocks the phone number just doesn't tell them. Just take down the number and do an investigation on it. You may find the phone number is linked to the debtor and give you new address information that you never had before. And if that doesn't work you have a phone number to start calling.

Reversing phone numbers is an evolving technology that many different skip trace databases stay on top of. Skipsmashers.com and Cellbust.com are a few different kinds of companies that you can go to for skip tracing. The first, being a searchable database with a few extra really nice features for getting an actual location on a cell phone. The latter being a hand search done by a seasoned skip tracer for a flat fee.

Bail Out

In most situations your assignments that come from an out of town finance company will require you to pay some out of pocket expenses and then tally those up with your final bill. In addition to fees charged that could include paying a bill to a mechanic's garage in order to take possession of the collateral. This is called a bail out.

A small percentage of people that get behind on their car note are debtors who refuse to pay a car note and repairs at the same time. True, they never tell the lien holder what's wrong with the car and it can just as well take many months for a debtor to tell you the truth about their car being in the shop. Certainly not until the debtor is talked out of it and the debtor knows that they can't get caught up on car payments and also pay the repair bills.

Repo Tools

Gate cards get left in most repos and I've over the years collected hundreds of cards. When I get to a gate I start going through my stack to open the gate, one after the other. When I get to one that opens the gate I write the name of the complex in a fine point sharpie on it so that I know next time which card to go for.

Getting into gates can be a long wait. If you're waiting for someone to go through the gate so that you can follow them inside an alternate move is to go in through the out gate. But you need a two man team to do this trick. Having a piece of metal on a rope from the front end of a car or a clip board with a metal clip, take the item and throw it past the sensor box.

You may have to throw for a couple of tried to get the gate open but once you do that person will need to stand by with that metal piece to continue to activate the sensor so that the gate won't close on your truck. Just don't let the gate shut on your car. Trust me when I say it leaves a huge dent.

Key codes for repossessions can be found in a couple of different ways. One of the ways is a vendor that sells key codes to you and another way is to take your repossession paperwork to the service department of a dealer and get a key cut that will only open the door.

The bigger your repo company gets, key making equipment would be an investment and be a convenience for your employees to be able to do this all important task right there in your own garage rather than take the collateral to another place to have it done, and bring it back.

There are two things that my repo trucks carry that my competitors don't have. The first thing is doggie snacks and the second is bolt cutters. Ok, my competition may have bolt cutters. Doggie snacks are smart though. If you drive past a house that has a bunch of dogs and a car behind a fence, those dogs will know and love you by the third visit.

Bacon, raw cubed stew meat is cheap at the grocery store, heck even Slim Jim's work. You're creating a bond beyond the dog and master when you intervene with some yummy puppy treat goodness. And you're not going to have any problems opening that gate and getting your repo.

Using your friends in a time of need is a good thing. There's been many times where I found my repo blocked in by another car that was just sitting up and never moved. Getting another repo truck to drag out the car blocking yours in is an alternate move. You should make it a very fast move, as in your buddy drags out and drops the car blocking in your on the side of the road and take off, so you can get your repo and take off.

If you're worried about video cameras catching you, use magnet sheets (like the ones that Vista Print sells) to cover your state letters and numbers on the side of your trucks and license plates. Also, spray your tires with a 50% Dawn and water solution to prevent the loud screeching sounds when dragging out a repo.

Another way to get a repo out of a tight spot is using go-jacks. These four-wheeled wonders go around a tire and are jacked up to lift the tire up off the ground so it can roll on the four smaller wheels on the go-jack. Great for getting cars out of garages where the battery has died or getting cars out of angled spots where you have no key and can't turn the steering wheel.

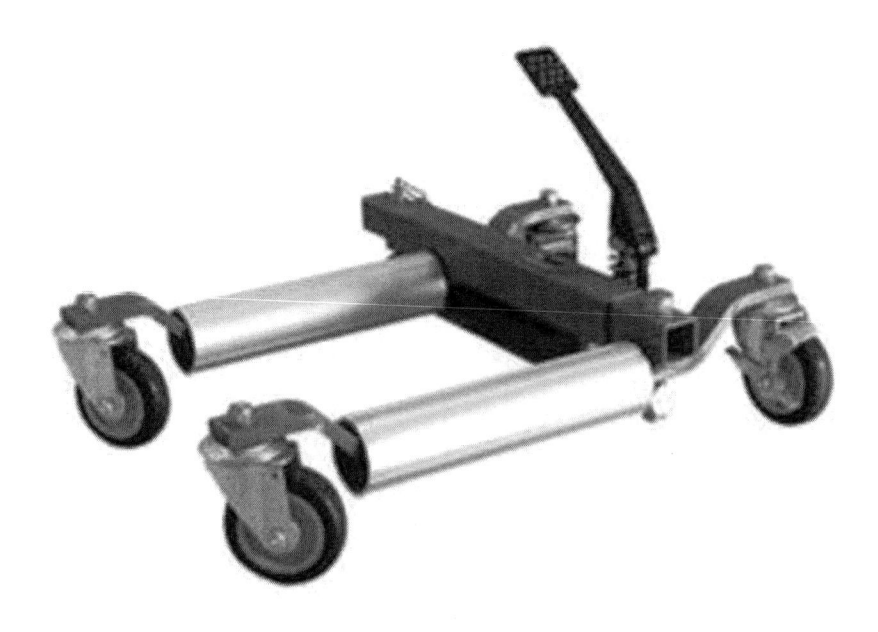

Forms

If your client has employment verification forms and residency verification forms in the file, those forms are good forever. If you suspect that a person is working for a particular company you can fax the request over to the human resource office and actually receive a response. Same goes for apartment complex management and other residential lease situations.

If you're a reposystems.com user preloaded into every repossession entry on your account will be forms that you can click and the software prints with all of the specific details of the debtor and collateral. Remember that user code is **Tw2J3 to get your discounts on signing up**.

RESIDENCY VERIFICATION FORM

Regarding:
Name: _____

Social Security: _____

Date of Birth: _____

To Whom It May Concern:
I, _____, certify that the following person(s):
(List the names of all residents)
_____
_____
_____

Reside at
_____
_____

Name of Leaseholder Mortgagee
_____
(If joint)
_____

Signature of Leaseholder/Mortgagee_____

Date signed_____

Transportation from your storage lot to a destination that your client designates. That could be to his storage lot, an auto auction or a third party that bought the collateral from your client.

TRASNPORTATION RELEASE

"Receipt is hereby given and acknowledged that on the above date, the AGENT signed below received and took possession of the above described collateral upon the order of the above referenced client. It is furthermore acknowledged that the AGENT signed below forever releases [YOUR COMPANY NAME] against any and all claims upon assuming possession of the collateral.

AGENT (PRINT) :_____
AGENT (SIGN) : _____
Date:_____

Alternate language for releasing the collateral to the debtor:

This vehicle can only be released to the debtor/registered owner or authorized client/auction transporter, as specified below.

The undersigned hereby acknowledges receiving and inspecting the vehicle described on this form and finding said vehicle to be in good condition and all personal property and keys accounted for and hereby releases [YOUR COMPANY NAME] and/or their clients and/or agents from any and all claims now and hereafter, whether known or unknown, anticipated or unanticipated.

Just remember to place the VIN number on all your forms with the debtor's name, the name of the client and the contact person for the client. You can also place your account number if you have software that gives another number besides using the VIN as an account number. If your client reconditions and resells the same unit, the previous debtor could come up in your system if you only input the VIN to search.

I never delete any previous debtors from my repo software system because in my city it's very likely that I would get the same debtor for a different client. Having the past information could help me get the next vehicle picked up.

Repo Laws by State

Alabama-This is a self-help repossession state. Debtor has ten days to redeem unit with a certified notice. So ten days free storage would be required by the client. There are no special licensing requirements for repossessions in Alabama. License plates remain with the debtor.

Alaska-This is a self-help repossession state. License plates remain with the vehicle with the exception of personalized license plates. Those remain with the debtor. Debtor can redeem in ten days, so ten days free storage would be required by the client.

Arizona-This is a self-help repossession state. The debtor can redeem within ten days so ten days free storage is required by client. There are no special repossession license requirements.

Arkansas-This is a self-help repossession state. The debtor can redeem within ten days, so ten days free storage is required by client. Vehicles that tow are required to be licensed by the Arkansas Towing and Recovery Board **http://www.artowing.org** License plates remain with the debtor.

California-This is a self-help repossession state. The debtor can redeem within fifteen days (15). Debtor must pay additional fee to police department to redeem. Repossession company must be licensed by Bureau of Security and Investigative Services Phone (916) 322-4000 License plates remain with the vehicle with the exception of personalized license plates, which stay with the owner.

Colorado-This is a self-help repossession state. The debtor has ten days to redeem the vehicle from the client. No license requirements but there is a repossessor bond required by the state and must be on file with the State Attorney General's office. (303) 866-4500 License plates remain with the owner.

Connecticut-This is a self-help repossession state. Must notify police department in advance of repossession in some towns. Debtor has 15 days to redeem and collateral must stay in state where repossessed. No special licensing for repossession agencies. License plates remain with debtor.

Delaware-This is a self-help repossession state. Debtor can redeem vehicle until unit is sold at auction and must pay loan all the way off. No licensing requirements for repossession agencies. License plates remain with collateral.

District of Columbia-This is a self-help repossession state. The state requires 15 days for the debtor to redeem the loan. Repossession licensing is required. License plates remain with the debtor.

Florida-This is a self-help repossession state with the exception of mobile homes. Debtor has ten days to redeem loan. Repossession agencies, individuals, skip trace personal all must be licensed with the state. Division of Licensing, Tallahassee, FL. License plates stay with the debtor.

Georgia-This is a self-help repossession state. The debtor has ten days to redeem the loan. Repossession insurance must be registered with the state. License plates stay with the debtor.

To find out the reported license plate, date and location of last emissions test:

http://www.cleanairforce.com/motorists/virreprints.php

Hawaii-This is a self-help repossession state. The debtor has ten days to redeem the loan. Repossession agencies are considered collection agencies and must have a license with the Commerce and Consumer Affairs. The license plates remain with the collateral.

Idaho-This is a self-help repossession state. Debtors have ten days to redeem the loan. No special repossession licensing requirements. License plates remain with the debtor.

Illinois-This is a self-help repossession state. Debtors can redeem vehicle anytime before unit is sold. Repossession license is granted by the Illinois Commerce Commission and license plates remain with the owner.

Indiana-This is a self-help repossession state. The debtor has ten days to redeem the loan. There are no special licensing requirements for repossession agencies. The license plates remain with the owner.

Iowa- This is a self-help repossession state but has a 21 day waiting period after the demand to pay current is sent to the debtor. Debtor has ten days to redeem loan. No repossession license requirements. License plates remain with the debtor.

Kansas-This is a self-help repossession state. Debtor has ten days to redeem loan. No repossession license requirements. License plates remain with the debtor.

Kentucky-This is a self-help repossession state. Debtor can redeem loan any time prior to repossession. There are no repossession license requirements. License plates remain with the debtor.

Louisiana-This is a self-help repossession state. If the words, "Louisiana no longer requires repossession with judicial process." Are a part of the contract, a self-help repossession is allowed. If these words are not a part of the contract then the debtor must voluntarily surrender the vehicle. There are no required time limits to redeem the loan. Repossession licenses are required with the Office of Financial Institutions in Baton Rouge, LA. (225) 925-4660. License plates must be returned to the state DMV.

Maine-This is a self-help repossession state. The debtor has ten days to redeem the loan. Repossession license is required through Bureau of Consumer Credit Protection (207) 624-8527. License plates remain with the debtor.

Maryland-This is a self-help repossession state. The debtor has fifteen days to redeem the loan. Repossession license is required by the Office of the Commissioner of Financial Regulation. License plates remain with the owner.

Massachusetts-Collateral cannot be repossessed from a home owned or rented by the debtor. The debtor has twenty days to redeem the loan. There are no license requirements for repossession agencies. License plates remain with the owner.

Michigan-This is a self help repossession state. The debtor has fifteen days to redeem the loan. A repossession license is obtained through the Department of Labor and Economic Growth. The license plates remain with the owner.

Minnesota-This is a self help repossession state. The debtor has ten days to redeem the loan. There is no license required for repossessions. License plates remain with the vehicle.

Mississippi-This is a self help repossession state. The debtor has ten days to redeem the loan. There is no license required for repossessions. License plates remain with the debtor.

Missouri-This is a self-help repossession state. A copy of the contract or title must be with the authorization to repossess. There are no requirements for a repossession license. License plates stay with the debtor, lease vehicles license plates stay with the vehicle.

Montana-This is a self help repossession state. Transport between counties requires a permit. Repossession is final remedy for collection on loans. The debtor has ten days to redeem the loan. There is no license required for repossession. License plates stay with the debtor.

Nebraska-This is a self help repossession state. The debtor has ten days to redeem the loan. There are no requirements for repossession license. License plates remain with the owner.

Nevada- This is a self help repossession state. The debtor has ten days to redeem the loan. Repossession agencies are licensed through the Nevada Attorney General's Office. License plates remain with the owner.

New Hampshire-This is a self help repossession state. The debtor has ten days to redeem the loan. There are no requirements for repossession license. License plates remain with the owner.

New Jersey-This is a self help repossession state. The debtor has ten days to redeem the loan. There are no requirements for repossession license. License plates remain with the owner.

New Mexico-This is a self help repossession state. The debtor has ten days to redeem the loan. Repossession agencies obtain a license through the New Mexico State Corporation Commission. License plates remain with the owner.

New York-This is a self help repossession state. The debtor has ten days to redeem the loan. There are no requirements for repossession license. License plates are returned to the DMV.

North Carolina-This is a self help repossession state. The debtor has ten days to redeem the loan. There are no requirements for repossession license. License plates remain with the owner.

North Dakota-This is a self help repossession state. The debtor has ten days to redeem the loan. There are no requirements for repossession license. License plates remain with the collateral.

Ohio- This is a self help repossession state. The debtor has ten days to redeem the loan. Repossession license can be obtained through the Bureau of Motor Vehicles (614) 752-7500. License plates remain with the owner.

Oklahoma- This is a self help repossession state. The debtor has twenty days to redeem the loan. Repossession license can be obtained from the Department of Public Safety Wrecker Services Division (405) 511-3221. License plates remain with the collateral.

Oregon- This is a self help repossession state. The debtor has ten days to redeem the loan. Repossession license can be obtained with the Division of Finance and Corporate Securities (503) 945-7924. License plates remain with the vehicle and personalized plates stay with the owner.

Pennsylvania- This is a self help repossession state. The debtor has fifteen days to redeem the loan. Repossession agencies must be registered with Pennsylvania Department of Banking, Licensing Division (717) 787-3717. License plates remain with the owner.

Rhode Island-This is a self help repossession state. The debtor has twenty days to redeem the loan. There are no requirements for repossession license. License plates are turned into the DMV.

South Carolina-This is a self help repossession state. The debtor has ten days to redeem the loan. There are no requirements for repossession license. License plates remain with the owner.

South Dakota-This is a self help repossession state. The debtor has ten days to redeem the loan. There are no requirements for repossession license. License plates remain with the collateral.

Tennessee-This is a self help repossession state. The debtor has ten days to redeem the loan. There are no requirements for repossession license. License plates remain with the owner.

Texas-This is a self help repossession state. The debtor has ten days to redeem the loan. There are no requirements for repossession license. License plates remain with the vehicle. Tow truck operators must be TDLR certified by the state and pass an exam and background check as no felonies would disallow a tow license.

Utah-This is a self help repossession state. The debtor doesn't have options to redeem the loan. There are no requirements for repossession license. License plates remain with the owner.

Vermont-This is a self help repossession state. The debtor can redeem until vehicle is sold. There are no requirements for repossession license. License plates remain with the owner or get turned into the state if unclaimed.

Virginia-This is a self help repossession state. The debtor has ten days to redeem the loan. There are no requirements for repossession license. License plates remain with the owner.

Washington-This is a self help repossession state. The debtor has ten to twenty one days to redeem the loan. Repossession agencies are licensed through the Department of Licensing (360) 902-3770. License plates remain with the owner.

West Virginia-This is a self help repossession state. There aren't any statutes allowing the debtor to redeem the loan. There are no requirements for repossession license. License plates stay with the vehicle with the exception of personalized plates, those stay with the debtor.

Wisconsin-This state requires a debtor to sign a voluntary surrender waiver or must obtain a court order to take possession of collateral. The debtor has fifteen days to redeem the loan. There are no requirements for repossession license. License plates remain with the owner.

Wyoming-This is a self help repossession state. The debtor has ten days to redeem the loan. There are no requirements for repossession license. License plates remain with the owner.

Recommended Reading

The Pretext Play Book
by James O'Reilly

Amzn.to/pretextplay

Find this where you buy your books and e-books.

Pretext in this book is dissected and put forth in a very careful manner so that the user has all precautions in place to not only protect his identity but to get the information set out to obtain in the pretext.

Skip Trace Secrets:
Dirty little tricks skip tracers use... by Valerie McGilvrey

LearnSkipTracing.com

Skip tracing is indeed an art and this book written by a skip tracer that specializes in repossession skip tracing has this art down to an exact science.

Here you'll learn all about the best databases that cater to the repo industry and truck loads of free resources that are little known outside the world of recovery. This book has amazing reviews and the author also keeps an up close and personal blog specifically for recovery folks like me and you.

The Complete Idiot's Guide to Private Investigating
by Steven Kerry Brown

Steven Brown has a great blog. He has a fantastic investigative mind and is a great teacher.

Steven also has followed and worked on some very high profile cases and shares his investigations with us along with his many golden nuggets. These links are for the third edition that was released in 2013. Look for newer editions of this book when buying.

Helpful Websites

Thedailyskip.com

Spokeo.com

Skipsmasher.com

3shark.net

Birthdatabase.com

Bounceapp.com

Untiny.me

Quickmaps.com

Bing.com/social

Topsy.com

Postpost.com

Findicons.com

Office.com

Whois.sc

Ewhois.com

Whoishostingthis.com

Google.com/adplanner

Downornot.com

Webs.com

Wix.com

Joliprint.com

Rdd.me

Everytimezone.com

Viewer.zoho.com

Spypig.com

Scr.im

Futureme.org

Ohlife.com

Regex.info

Join.me

Efax.com

Myfax.com

Repoman.com

Thedailyskip.com

Deadurl.com

Feedmyinbox.com

Ctrlq.org/html-mail

10minuitemail.com

Disposablewebpage.com

Screenr.com

Dabbleboard.com

Docusign.com

Echosign.com

Google.com/cloudprint

Bing.com/twitter/maps

Letter.ly

http://www.deathindexes.com/cemeteries.html

Glossary

Self-help:

The unpleasant and integral part of motor finance where repossession is the main remedy that a creditor has to guard against a total loss. It also means no court order to repossess and a lien holder can repossess collateral themselves without having to pay a repossessor licensed or not.

Sequestration:

A court order granting the lien holder possession of the collateral. Legally called a Writ of Sequestration. When police departments tell you that you must have a writ to take possession in certain circumstances this is what they refer to. The precursor to the Writ is that the debtor must be served first and usually this is impossible to accomplish before locating the debtor.

Collateral:

The tangible object that is the secured interest of the loan. Such as a sewing machine, car, boat or trailer.

Ping:

To send a signal to a device and receive a physical location.

Triangulation:

The digital path of a cellular phone transmission between cell phone towers transmitting to the cell phone.

Made in the USA
Middletown, DE
01 December 2014